Tina

Breathe in
the good —
Exhale all
the bullshit

xoxo
denise

Your Relationship

with

You

Your Relationship

with

HOW TO LIVE LIFE
BY YOUR RULES

DENISE C. ONOFREY, LMFT, CST

THE RELATIONSHIP STRATEGIST

To my parents, clients & mentors

Contents

ABOUT THE BOOK

My passion is people. As corny as it reads at first glance, it is truly the underpinning of my heart and soul, my philosophy as a relationship therapist and my approach to how I live and work. And one of the things I love most about people is our connectedness—our relationships with each other.

From early in my career as a sex and relationship therapist in Denver, Colorado, I found the majority of clients' issues were related to a lack of connection. For some clients, this was a lifelong struggle, while for others it was due to changes in their relationships and family dynamics. Health, aging, career, and community changes also impacted my clients' quality of connection. Lack of connection from self and others manifests in a vast number of ways, such as ineffective communication, depression, lack of sexual desire, substance abuse, decreased motivation, loneliness, frustration, isolation, anger, hopelessness, and a sense of helplessness. After years of seeing this pattern persist, I began designing specific strategies for clients to experience connection with themselves while working to recreate and enrich connection within their intimate relationships.

Connection is not only essential for survival, but for enrichment and pleasure, too; where there is connection, there is ease.

So why are we so disconnected from each other, and why are relationships so hard at times? For one thing, relationships are hard because we aren't exactly inundated with know-how. We often lack strong and consistent relationship role models; when we look to cultural messages thrust upon us from TV, marketing, and media, we learn that relationships are supposed to be easy, breezy and without strife. So when reality brings discord and difficulty we are not only confused, but we often remain secretive about it because of the shame of not getting it "right." Even worse, we often cover our shame with a need to display a pretended perfection—we throw a smile on and hope things will get better. Of course they don't.

Too often the clients I have worked with have tried everything to improve their quality of life and relationships without considering the significance of connection to themselves first. The expectation is that we should be in relationships, with ourselves and with others, but there is scant information telling us how to do so.

We are making relationships harder than they need to be. Our culture supports and encourages us *having* a relationship, but does not provide much by way of understanding the inner workings of healthy, connected and easier relationships. As a sex and relationship therapist, I have been privy to the inner workings of many relationships—I really do know what is going on in your neighbor's marriage and in their bedroom. I come to you with years of insight into why relationships are in the state they are, how we got to where we are, and what to do about it.

This is Book One of The Connection Strategy Book Series, a three-part series. The purpose of the series is to provide you a resource for more connected and easier relationships. Book One, the one you now hold in your hands, is about YOU. It's a way to enrich, relearn (or learn for the first time) those life lessons you deserve in order to forge a more connected and easier relationships with YOURSELF. Book One will transform you into someone who knows how to have and create connection and ease because you will have formed a relationship of connection and ease with *yourself*. We would all have easier and more connected relationships with spouses, partners, children, and colleagues if we sought the same desired qualities, meaning and purpose within ourselves prior to seeking relationships with others.

Book Two, "We: Relationship Strategies for Connection," will help you use the tools you learn here in Book One to establish healthy relationship patterns and practices with others, including romantic partnerships.

Book Three, "Me: The Pleasure of Being a Woman," honors the sexual self. It not only helps add desire but also helps you get in touch with your erotic, sexual, and sensual self. Each book in The Connection Strategy Book Series stands alone as a practical course in making relationships more connected and easier, but together the books serve as a comprehensive go-to reference.

Importantly—and please note this carefully—these books are NOT for relationships with active addiction, active abuse, active affairs, or major secrets. When we have these big, unresolved issues in ourselves or our relationships, we MUST treat these issues first, then go back and fine-tune with the strategies in these books. If any of these issues are active in your life, please seek life-changing and life-saving professional help. A good resource for finding licensed and qualified professionals is PsychologyToday.com.

MY STORY

By reading *Your Relationship with You: How to Live Life by Your Rules* I want you to make your own rules, to buck the system, and question the status quo in your life. Without doing this, we risk failing to discover and examine our truest self, to connect with that self and have quality connection to others. Until I got clear on the rules for my truest self, I lived life by someone else's rules. I was striving to fit into what our culture told me I was supposed to be, do, say, feel and pursue. I wasn't happy, productive, or fulfilled.

The rules I followed were clear from the beginning. I wanted to be a mother and have a white picket fence. As a child, I knew very few women who weren't mothers and I had few role models outside this norm. Like most children, I had little exposure to options other than what I saw before me. In other words, there were a handful of "must-follow" rules which I could not see beyond.

In my high school years, I believed I needed to "couple up," to keep the same boyfriend because I believed long-term relationships were ideal. As a young adult in college, my world and possibilities began to open up ever so slightly. Freedom, choice, diversity, options and wonder ran parallel to questioning the status quo and experiencing myself in a larger context. I could stretch out a bit, and try on different versions of myself. I began to experience making my own rules based on my relationship with myself as an individual. However, I had yet to develop any real strategies to embrace my truest self.

Fast forward a bit—I got married in my early twenties. I was living under the illusion that obtaining the M words was the only way to follow the rules: first "Man," then "Marriage," and next, according to the rule book, "Motherhood." Getting married was a box I had to check to validate myself, my decisions, and my future. It was as if I had to cross that item off the Get Life Right checklist. I had "known" from an early age that being partnered up, being a girlfriend and then a wife is how I would become a real woman.

Two years into my marriage I woke up in the middle of the night, sat straight up in bed and said out loud, "Oh no!" I was sleeping next to one of the most generous, kind, loving, understanding souls I ever knew, but I suddenly realized I could not be the mother of his children and he could not be the father of mine. I left that marriage.

I left it ungracefully, abruptly, immaturely, painfully, and shamefully. I never looked back because I couldn't bear to see what I had done. I remember thinking, "Where do I learn about being in relationships as opposed to only learning I should be in one?"

It happened again in 2008. I woke up in the middle of the night, sat straight up in bed and said out loud, "Oh no!" I thought of those non-existent children I left my marriage for. I was in my early thirties and I realized I might never be a mother. But this time, instead of reacting ungracefully as I had before or feeling defeated because of the inability to fulfill yet another series of milestones and rules, I asked myself, "If you could live life by your own rules, what would those rules be?"

No-brainer! I would become a therapist with a private practice in the business of relationships. Finally! I had my own uncharted territory to navigate: my rules, my success.

We are all shaped by our surroundings, by spoken and unspoken rules, our culture, our perceptions of what we are supposed to be, to do, to say, to feel, and to pursue. I wrote this book because I want each of us to have the opportunity to step back, to explore and to discover the rules we have been following; rules that no longer serve us. I want you to design your own way to show up and live your life. Lastly, I want each of us to add and eliminate factors keeping us from living the life we were intended to live. I want us all to be more empowered to buck the system—the usual, the rut, the daily grind—we all fall into by trying to get it right according to somebody else's rules.

My mission has long been to help each of us better indulge in the finer things in life: relationships, connection, and ease. When we eliminate factors that create noise and distraction, as well as when we add key strategies to live with more connection and ease, our relationships will truly be our greatest asset. I am speaking about all types of relationships: parents, children, lovers, friends, neighbors, and community. At the end of the day, our riches come from the people around us; let's create key strategies to indulge in those riches more fully. But first, we must start with the relationship we have with ourselves.

WHERE WE ARE HEADED

Chapter One: When Life Has a Different Plan Than You Did
We have all said "this is not what I had planned," which can leave us feeling lost, dissatisfied, defeated and drained. Most of us are not exposed to, or influenced by, the truths of working relationships, including how to be in a relationship with ourselves. Your relationship with yourself is the key to connection and ease with others. It is also the key to designing your Plan B.

Chapter Two: Where Did That Plan A Come From Anyway? Design Your Plan by Your Rules
We are all shaped by rules and expectations and not every rule we have been following is ideal for us. We all have at least one area of life that did not turn out as planned, which can leave us stuck and disconnected. It is time for us to write our own rules for life.

Chapter Three: Slow and Calm Wins the Race
We must slow down, explore, and set a course with a fresh view of our history as well as our current state of affairs if we are to live by our own rules. In addition, we must address the not-so-healthy habits we have developed to deal with the stress and overwhelm of things not going as planned. We must calm to connect.

Chapter Four: An Emotion Decoder Ring

It is essential we understand our emotions and related needs prior to expecting someone else to do the same. The formula is simple: first we calm the self, next we get clear about the self, and then we connect to the self.

Chapter Five: That Stuff We Do to Tune Out

Examine the habits and ruts you have fallen into that distract you from what is happening in and around you. These include any distracting habits outside of moderation such as drinking, shopping, gambling, and Facebooking. These distractions are keeping you from your truest self, therefore hindering your connection with yourself and others. We all engage in self-soothing behaviors, but beware of unsustainable habits and distractions.

Chapter Six: Psst! Your Gut Has Something to Say

People-pleasing and perfectionism are the most effective ways to quiet your gut reaction. The sad thing is, your gut reaction is the voice of your truest self. We must learn to harness the innate wisdom of our gut. Without the skill of knowing when, where, and to whom we should say no, people-pleasing and perfectionism are writing your rules. We can be stuck with resentments and feel drained and overwhelmed by demands that don't feed our truest self.

Chapter Seven: Chuck It in the F*&#-It Bucket

Oh yes, "The Bucket." This is an extremely popular strategy because it is simple, significant, and helps you decipher who and what deserves YOU. The Bucket is the boundary to put between you and what drains you.

Chapter Eight: Getting Your Brain In On It

We need brain accessing strategies to build more of what we want and prune what isn't working. The good news is once we get our brain in on the job, it's like having a superhero who seems to just get things done with little effort.

Chapter Nine: You're Just a Tall Baby!

Let's get clear on what it means to be human by going back to the basics. This strategy provides the language, insights, and thinking points to help you understand yourself and those around you. Every one of us is a "Tall Baby."

Chapter Ten: Intentionally You by <u>Your</u> Rules

What's next for you? Where is your time, energy, and purpose going to be invested? What rules are you going to live by to maintain calm and clarity, to create and enrich more connection and easier relationship with you? Once we get the relationship with the self more connected and easier, we can turn toward others for connection and ease.

WHEN LIFE HAS A DIFFERENT PLAN THAN YOU DID

Nobody comes to my office where I see private clients in Denver, Colorado because they are inundated with the rainbows and butterflies of life. Oftentimes clients come to me because they are experiencing a rut in their life or relationship while recognizing "This is not what I had planned." Clients feel lost, dissatisfied, defeated, and drained from their previous attempts to do whatever it takes to maintain their Plan A. My clients find themselves in a circumstance, chapter, or experience they had not planned for and don't know how to move on from.

This foreign land often inspires few solutions, and without solutions, we get stuck. Even worse, we can blindly choose the closest Plan B, but without adequate self-examination, we will eventually return to dissatisfaction. Oftentimes we seek solutions externally, blame others, or lament the loss of the Plan A we had counted on.

Whether single or married for four years or 40 years, it has been my experience clients usually find life had a different plan for them than they had envisioned. Here's a hint as to why: most of us are not exposed to or influenced by the truths of working relationships, including how to be in a relationship with ourselves. Without this knowledge, we cannot create a sustainable plan nor set the rules we live by with optimal outcomes

I am as optimistic as they come, but I am also realistic. Relationships are hard. And at the risk of being a complete downer, LIFE IS HARD. Yet I see how we are making both relationships and life harder than necessary.

Nobody can honestly say, "My life is exactly as planned." Sure, you got your MBA, you traveled to interesting places, had a kiddo or two—all or some of these events were in The Plan. But we have all experienced life's little (or big) earthquakes, where life has pulled the rug out from under us and we are spinning in the air, not knowing which end is up. Divorce, infertility, professional stagnation, unexpected death of a loved one, infidelity, and unexpected health issues are all real-life examples from my clients. These life earthquakes shake our core and demand a change of plan, a recalibration, and a forging ahead.

When the unexpected life earthquake shakes us up, we can easily become stuck because we are in new territory. We are equipped with only so many resources. We turn to friends, Dr. Phil and those like him, books like this one, and a myriad of other hoped-for solutions. Some people never attempt to fix the stuckness at all, but rather live in that space for a time, sometimes for a long time. The latter is truly heartbreaking because the silence and inaction is likely due to shame, to not knowing, and to the fear of being found out: the fear and shame of others knowing that our life isn't so great behind closed doors. Even worse, if we can't find a solution to our woes, we often resort to blaming external factors. This diminishes our relationship with ourselves and inhibits our potential to find solutions within.

This chapter launches us into acknowledging where things are not going as planned and positions us to write new rules for our life. To prevent merely falling into Plan B by default, it is important to slow down, examine, access your own wisdom, and eliminate what no longer belongs in your rules. Let's start laying the foundation for your new rules by taking an honest look at where you are today.

When I reflect on my life I did not expect:

*being where I am today, single
divorced, no career, business
struggling, unhappy, discontent
and full of fear of being
alone*

As I embark on creating change in my life and/or relationship, I would like to add the following to my life and/or relationship:

*joy in my own self
being happy single
thriving business
to love myself first*

As I embark on creating change in my life and/or relation-ship, I know it would be wise for me to eliminate the following habits, people, stressors, drains, etc:

negative thinking
shameful behavior

If I had a magic wand to create the life I want, my life would feel (keyword-feel!): Here are "feeling" words to help you gain awareness about how you want your life to feel. Choose all that fit.

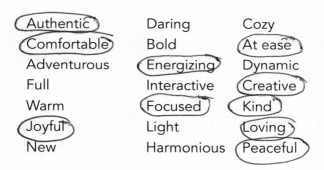

(Authentic)	Daring	Cozy
(Comfortable)	Bold	(At ease)
Adventurous	(Energizing)	Dynamic
Full	Interactive	(Creative)
Warm	(Focused)	(Kind)
(Joyful)	Light	(Loving)
New	Harmonious	(Peaceful)

What more do you want your life to feel like?

loving
fulfilled

Despite not everything turning out as planned in my life and/or relationship, I am grateful for:

the 3 boys I had and finding Jesus

In Chapter One, we have set the course for self-exploration—for understanding ourselves better in order to have more connected and easier relationships. We have acknowledged that our lives did not turn out exactly as planned. In Chapter Two, we will explore where your Plan A came from in the first place and we will explore ways to create new rules for making an ideal Plan B.

Key Learning:

- We have all said, "This is not what I had planned," which can leave us feeling lost, dissatisfied, defeated, and drained.
- Most of us are not exposed to, or influenced by, the truths of working relationships, including how to be in a relationship with ourselves.
- Our relationship with ourself is the key to connection and ease with others.

2

WHERE DID THAT PLAN A COME FROM ANYWAY? DESIGN YOUR PLAN BY <u>YOUR</u> RULES

The truth is, nearly everyone is living a life different from what they imagined or hoped for. If they can't say this is true for at least one aspect of their life, they aren't telling the whole story. It is important to investigate how we arrived at that original Plan A in order to move forward with information, awareness, and discernment. If we continue to blindly fall into our next plan, we will continue the same patterns of stuckness again and again.

How did you get to this place of "Hmmm, this is not what I truly wanted," "This is not what I planned," or "I would have never chosen this path if I knew then what I know now?" What if there actually is no true way or plan? What if we needed to be blazing our own trail all this time? What if we were supposed to be in charge from the beginning?

Maybe this is why we arrived at this place of dissatisfaction. Maybe the problem is that we have been following someone else's plan. The most obvious "someone else's" are the adults who raised us and the environment in which our roots began. For the most part, our caregivers did the best they could with what they had and what they knew. Our caregivers (and their caregivers), our cultural norms, environment, family rules, and expectations, all provide us with essential insights to answer these questions: "So, how did I get here?" and "Why am I so disconnected and ill at ease in some areas of my life?" This isn't about finding the bad guy, blaming who raised us, or making a list of regrets or decisions. The first order of business is to look at the various systems that inform us, our decisions, our plans, and our life goals so we can best design and live life by our own rules. Let's look at my clients "Sarah" and "William."

Clients often enter therapy ready to hand over the reins to a professional. They arrive unsure of what else to do. They seek change and hope. My job is to uncover what each person brings to the relationship such as worldview, how each is "wired" by family of origin, and life experiences. Through targeted questioning as well as taking in every piece of a person's narrative, I begin to understand what it is like for each person to be in the relationship. I envision each person sitting at a table together, creating a unique space in the world that is their own. Throughout the work with each couple, I use the metaphor of the "Relationship Table" to highlight that they each bring something to the relationship—their union is a unique experience only they can have. The Relationship Table is also a place to leverage the uniqueness of the couple in order to investigate, create change, and reunite. I describe the Relationship Table to my clients as their "sacred space." This description invariably gives the couple a sense of empowerment, validation, and a powerful inner knowing that is a critical step along the path toward greater connection and ease.

Explore the System Then Buck It

As I tell my clients, with a few exceptions, we all had at least one halfway decent parent, caregiver, or adult in our childhood. These halfway decent caregivers molded us and shaped us based on their upbringing and how they were molded and shaped. There are overt and covert rules and expectations from which we set a course on how we would live, be in relationships, and parent. One of those clients, Sarah, was shaped, at eight years old, by the significant event of her mother dying because of poor health choices. Her mother's death shaped Sarah's rules about being a good parent, a good woman and wife, as well has how important health choices were for her and those around her. Sarah's Plan A was to do everything better than her mother. Sarah also did not want her children to suffer the same losses she had endured as a child. The covert rule Sarah learned was, in order to be a good mother, her children came first, at all costs, including before the needs of her husband, and even, ironically, her own health. Sarah invested time, money and energy in fulfilling her "how to be a good mother" rule. Though we can see how Sarah's beliefs may have been somewhat skewed by her mother's death, there are no major alarm bells going off. Sarah's intentions are admirable and she has two children who are loved and tended to.

However, Sarah's Plan A negatively interacted with her husband's Plan A. Sarah's husband of 18 years, William, was molded and shaped from his parenting and he learned the covert rule that spouses come first; all else comes second. It's a valid and acceptable expectation, no major alarm bells go off, right? However, the two Plan As are in opposition to each other. This intersection of two distinct rules created a rut in Sarah and William's marriage as they navigated decisions about quality time, family rules, and expectations. The couple had to accept they were automatically on Plan B simply by the nature of being together. Remember: Sarah: "kids first always" William: "spouses first, kids second." Sarah and William struggled for years as they both sought to fulfill their family (of origin) rules and expectations. Keep in mind too that as individuals, we are dynamic and complex. In the example of Sarah and William, they each come to their Relationship Table with thousands, of covert and overt family rules and expectations. These rules and expectations molded and shaped who they are and how they make sense of their relationships, family, and how the world works.

Through the process of honest self-examination, Sarah and William achieved a deeper understanding of themselves, the origins of their personal beliefs, and what each brings to the Relationship Table. This allowed the couple to rewrite their rules for the sake of their marriage. Sarah had to learn to cope with the anxiety of not always being the perfect mom. Perfectionism was woven into the rules and expectations of her family of origin. Sarah was able to explore this perfectionism more readily once we uncovered how perfectionism was detrimental to her relationship with herself, her children, and William. Sarah was also able to challenge her perfectionism in body image, health and household tasks.

William had to learn to cope with not always being first with his spouse, which is realistic at times, isn't it? William confronted his rigid black-and-white thinking that created a false sense of control and assurance. William's family-of-origin rules and expectations told him that if his wife wavered from this rule, he became unimportant, unlovable, and insignificant. This was a negative core belief William struggled with across many areas of his life and he discovered that the exploration with Sarah in couple's counseling generalized to others areas of his life. Sarah and William learned to resist fighting for Plan A (their typical interactional pattern based on lessons they learned from their upbringings), and began to explore their relationship's Plan B with a greater understanding of themselves, each other, and how to navigate together with more awareness. The result was more connection and ease with the self by confronting perfectionism and negative core beliefs. This armed each of them with more know-how as they turned toward each other in relationship.

We have only discussed *one* rule within *one* area of what shapes Sarah and William's Plan A. By examining expectations and the overt and covert rules from which we all come, we are much better equipped to write our own rules to live by.

Here is a sample of other areas Sarah and William explored in their couples counseling. I encourage you to explore your own roots as you learn about Sarah and William.

- Gender Expectations
  - Sarah: Family expectations were divided by gender. Girls were encouraged to be social, learn to have hobbies like dance, crafts and playing house, while her brothers were encouraged to be athletic and good students. Sarah's brothers weren't encouraged to be social, but rather be the best athletes in their community.
  - William: Family was egalitarian in which both genders had the same expectations. William's sister was a star tennis player and golfer, while William was encouraged to hone the culinary skills inherited from his mother.

These rules and expectations from their families of origin influence how Sarah and William parent their children. Once these issues were put on the Relationship Table, both Sarah and William realized that these truths, or rules, influenced the rules they conveyed to their children.

What gender rules or expectations shaped what you planned for your life?

- Educational/Professional Expectations
  - Sarah: Grew up in a home in which her brothers were expected to attend college, but Sarah had the choice to attend or not.
  - William: Family of origin had the expectations each child would attend college and a post-graduate program.

While examining this aspect of their roots, William was engaged in the conversation and had clarity around the opposing rules he and Sarah grew up with. However, at the end of the conversation he stated, "But my kids will be doctors or lawyers, I'd say." There it is again, that black-and-white thinking William engages in to create a false sense of control and assurance.

It is important for us to be graceful with ourselves and others as we examine our roots and, potentially, while bucking the system. Perhaps William will stay with this rule, perhaps not—it remains to be seen. However, consider the effects on the quality of connection and ease with his children if William maintains his black-and-white thinking. His children may want to be artists or teachers. Then what? What will they have learned from William's black-and-white thinking? How will his rigidity affect their ability to make their own plan?

What education and career rules or expectations shaped what you planned for your life?

- Financial Expectations:
  - Sarah: Childhood household was financially stable and conservative with spending.
  - William: Childhood household was liberal with spending despite financial instability. The family lived by the philosophy "You can't take it with you."

Sarah and William had difficulty throughout their relationship regarding finances. Through the process of examining rules and expectations they began to understand the "problem" wasn't the other person, but rather they each came to the Relationship Table with ingrained rules and expectations about money. By the way, William was also able to relate his childhood financial instability to his expectation that his children would become lawyers or doctors.

What financial and money rules or expectations shaped what you planned for your life?

- Parenting Expectations
  - Sarah: Children first, all else second
  - William: Spouse first, children second

What parenting rules or expectations shaped what you planned for your life?

- Home/Lifestyle Expectations
  - Sarah: The home is open to all, social gatherings were abundant, the home is humble and warm.
  - William: Socializing was typically maintained within the family with few family friends. Tidiness was not important.

What home and lifestyle rules or expectations shaped what you planned for your life?

- Body-image/Health Expectations
  - Sarah: Childhood was dominated by mother's illness and early death.
  - William: Childhood included healthy eating, exercise and conscious choices.

What body image rules or expectations shaped what you planned for your life?

- Religion/Community Expectations
  - Sarah: Grew up in Catholic family and attended Catholic schools.
  - William: Grew up with no exposure to religion and had little involvement in community outside of the family, sports leagues, and academic pursuits.

What religion/community rules or expectations shaped what you planned for your life?

Consider the six areas of expectations listed above. Which rules and expectations do you abide by that are working for you?

Consider the six areas of expectations listed above. Which rules and expectations do you abide by that are creating distress or turmoil?

There are a vast number of rules and expectations we follow that influence every aspect of our relationships, parenting, and worldview. It is essential to examine the rules you have been following in the areas of your life you wish to change. Examining rules is a personal process of reflection, being curious and open to possibility. In order to write new rules to live by, you must be aware and examine the rules in place that are causing distress or turmoil. Once you have identified an area in which you would like to create change, identify the rules that shaped this area. List all the rules and expectations you can think of. Keep an ongoing list and return to it often. When we open ourselves up to this type of personal reflection and examination, new thoughts will likely pop up when we are engaged in an unrelated activity. Once you have identified the rules and expectations that have shaped you, the next step is to notice how these rules contribute to your stuckness and dissatisfaction. The following chapters will provide you strategies to create and leverage your new awareness and support you in how to write new rules to live by.

Key Learning:
- ◆ We are all shaped by family-of-origin rules and expectations.
- ◆ Not every rule we have been following works for us in the present day.
- ◆ We all have at least one area of life that did not turn out as planned.
- ◆ Examining the rules and expectations we have been following offers insight into where we can create new rules and get unstuck.

3

SLOW AND CALM WINS THE RACE

If you picked up this book, you are seeking a change in some facet of your life. Maybe things aren't going as well as you intended, hoped, or planned. You may feel stuck, overwhelmed, isolated, ashamed, or angry. At this point, maybe you think you've tried everything, or perhaps this book is your first attempt to take the reins and create change. The first phase of change is typically a basic awareness of an issue and its components, or at least the distress related to the issue. Typically, my clients begin our work together remarking, "Something just isn't right, I can't do it like this anymore, help me discover more." Whether you are reading this book fully aware of what needs to change (work, marriage, sex, rat race, care for self, etc.), or you are reading this book to discover more about yourself and the components of your life, we are all arriving at this moment with the awareness that something isn't quite right or is not going as planned.

Beyond some simple perspective shifts and "If I knew then what I know now" insights, the strategy portion of this book provides you the opportunity to slow down, to continue to explore and to set a course with your own fresh view of where you've been, where you are, and where you are headed, all with your own rules. It is essential to balance this new learning with an awareness of the not-so-healthy habits (or strategies) we all pick up to deal with the stress of things not going as planned. Not-so-healthy habits can include equal (though opposite) behaviors of either overdoing or under-doing, and sometimes both. Chapter Five is devoted to this topic.

Our state of mind determines our connection, which informs our interactions, relationships, and experiences. If we're not calm, we're not connecting. Calm is the foundation of connecting with ourselves, and therefore helping us connect with others. *We must experience and learn to tap into calm as needed for optimal outcomes.* Re-read the last sentence and consider it from a child-rearing perspective! Parents know that self-soothing is a cornerstone of a baby's development. Well, guess what? As an adult, you need to revisit self-soothing skills for optimal outcomes. I have never been connected or intimate with anyone when I've been too stressed, too hungry, too tired, or too overwhelmed. The essential learning is that it is nobody else's responsibility to calm us, just as we are solely responsible for the quality of connection in our lives. Here are key strategies to strengthen calming states and healthy habits.

Strategy One: Your Calm Minute

Using your imagination to create calm offers a highly effective dose of emotional health and regulation. Imagine a place in the world, real or fictitious, a place where you are calm and serene. It is where you're at your finest, most at-ease, where you go with the flow. Practice pretending you're in this place one minute a day. It can be Fiji, it can be holding a sleeping, beautiful baby, anywhere real or imagined, for one minute a day.

My client "Heather," a successful realtor and mother of two, uses this highly effective calming technique when she sits at a red light while driving to property showings or getting her children from point A to point B: She imagines herself being on a chairlift at a ski resort. Heather is bucking the system and creating her own rules by calming herself, instead of turning to her phone to return a text or update her Facebook status about how busy she is. To achieve this, Heather simply recalls the sensory information related to skiing: the sights, sounds, smells, textures, temperature, and lighting in her calm place. Heather practices being in her calm place every chance she gets because she can't physically get up to the mountains as often as she would like. The funny thing is, for as savvy as our brains are, they can easily be tricked into experiencing just about anything.

Some call it meditation or daydreaming; call it whatever you want. I call it "Your Calm Minute." YCM is a practice of recalling and bringing in all of the sensory information related to a real or imagined place that inspires calm for one minute a day. This will give you an opportunity to take a break from your go-go-go-ness, from feeling stressed and overwhelmed. Our brains love calm; therefore, I want you to be practicing YCM every day. Set a timer and go to a beach in Fiji or to a ski slope. Imagine holding a beautiful child, a kitten, or a loved one. It's calm to connect. When we are calm, we connect. Practice this strategy when you don't need it, so you can more easily go to your calm place in moments you need it most.

Strategy Two: Do Nothing

It is essential to give ourselves quality and quiet alone time even if we only have one minute. In order to be connected to ourselves and others, we must experience *doing nothing.* Doing nothing means no phone, no music, no books; doing nothing means to sit and literally do nothing. Moms, CEOs, business travelers, single parents, and entrepreneurs alike initially scoff at my suggestion, and say something like my client Heather once said: "Rrrrright! Do nothing. What's that? I can't imagine, there is too much to do." She now practices "Doing Nothing" every morning with her cup of coffee. Our culture does not support us slowing down and doing nothing, so buck the system and find a time of day that works for you. Do nothing.

We cannot fully be our best selves without experiencing ourselves, hearing our own thoughts, and checking with our own gut feelings. Slowing down to check in with what our gut feels offers far more connection than any amount of thinking. Thinking is overrated when it comes to calming ourselves. After working with hundreds of clients behind closed doors, I have found that too many of us rely on external soothing methods to distract us from our internal emotional experience (we explore this more in Chapter Four). Without connecting with ourselves, we rely too heavily on others—our spouses, friends, and even our children—to achieve a calm and soothed state. The essential learning is that we are our own best caregivers. We can provide ourselves optimal calm, which allows us to show up to our partner, our children, and the community more complete and able to connect authentically, which will enrich our calm and connection. Doing Nothing is an essential practice: Set a timer for at least one minute and do nothing but hear yourself, check in with your senses, and breathe.

Our emotional response to slowing down creates resistance to writing our own rules related to calm and bucking the system of our go-go-go culture. Guilt and fear of missing out are common responses that surface when I attempt to do nothing or slow down. Next come the thoughts of "I should be_____." Even in this moment, as I write the very book in your hands, I am wondering if emptying the dishwasher would be a better use of my time (Sheesh! I don't even really care about the dishes. It seems to be a battle of efficient use of time). Once I refocus on the writing, parts of my mind work to convince the "dishwasher thinking parts" that writing is in fact the best use of my time. It can feel like a battle in my head and I am the only person who can make a change for myself. Once the emotions and thoughts start to race, which feels like both a sprint and a marathon, the physical sensations become noticeable. In this moment I am sitting in my comfy home, on my couch I refer to as "The Nest." I have coffee poured, candles lit, there is a chilly and cloudy day outside the window, and yet I notice I am not physically calm. I am slightly agitated and ill at ease. My logical self does not get what is happening, but it is real. This type of experience reminds me that Doing

Nothing will serve me better than getting words on a page or emptying the dishwasher.

If we're not calming, we're not connecting. Calm is the foundation to connecting with ourselves, and therefore helping us connect with others. *We must experience and learn to tap into calm as needed for optimal outcomes.* Noticing emotional reactions will inform us when we need to practice one of these strategies. Also, these strategies will be more effective when we need them if we have consistently practiced them beforehand.

Key Learning:
- Our state of mind determines our connection, which informs our interactions, relationships, and experiences.
- Slowing down provides opportunity to explore and hear ourselves.
- We can leverage our imaginations to achieve a calm state.
- Slowing down can create a negative emotional response such as guilt because our culture does not support us slowing down.
- If we do not calm, we will not connect.

AN EMOTION DECODER RING

Our emotions must be honestly investigated, accurately named, and fully understood in order to embrace what we are experiencing and needing. However, we are often too limited in our words to accurately name and understand our internal emotional experience. As a result, we cannot fully understand our needs, leaving our truest needs unmet. With these limitations, we cannot create our truest rules to live by or create our ideal Plan B. Remember, if we blindly choose or fall into our Plan B, then we are destined to repeat old patterns of stuckness and dissatisfaction. To take the bold step of living life by our own rules, we must decode our emotions and their related needs. When we have a deeper understanding of our emotional experiences, we are one major step closer to clarifying our needs and getting those needs met.

Emotions are the most reliable source of deciphering our needs, and each of us must be able to articulate our needs for more connection and ease. A constant stream of emotion runs throughout our days and we can get stuck in some of these emotions. Working to identify emotions and learning what they are telling us will prevent us from getting stuck in an unpleasant spot for too long. When we have an emotional experience, logic seems to fly out the window; we may lose ground, lose perspective, and seem to lose the ability to escape feeling stuck. This emotional merry-go-round can keep us disconnected and we certainly aren't going to experience ease in our relationships. The essential learning here is we must look at the relationship we have with ourselves; we must understand our emotions and needs prior to expecting someone else to do the same. How do we do that? First, we calm the self. Then we get clear. Finally, we connect. Let's start with clarity and emotions.

Emotions. We avoid them, fake them, suppress them, and distract ourselves from our most important emotional experiences. We experience multiple emotions at one time. It is fascinating to me that when asked, "How are you?" we seem to have the automatic response of sugarcoating our truth. My client "Jack," husband, father, physician, and triathlete, has been experimenting with his immediate response and sharing the truth of his internal emotional experience with his wife "Lisa." It has NOT been easy and not always well-received. He continues to plug away at creating change in his relationships, including the one he has with himself, by more accurately labeling and verbalizing his emotions. The results have, at minimum, provided him

YOUR RELATIONSHIP WITH *You*

with insight into who is truly available for a more connected relationship and who is seeking the quality of connection he is also seeking.

Yes, there are certain people and occasions with whom and where we should probably use social or professional norms to answer more generally. However, this book is about our most intimate and supposedly safest relationships. When we are not articulating our truest selves and our truest experiences, we are missing an opportunity to connect to ourselves and others. One of the first tools I use with my clients is the "Emotion Word List" to help them identify their emotions more accurately. Oftentimes I ask, "so, how does that/do you feel?" and if the response is "OK," "fine," or "good," I teasingly threaten to get out the Emotion Word List. I find that when using the word list, clients discover just the right words to describe their emotional experience. Better yet, clients will begin to notice a pattern of where and when the same emotions arise.

Once we can identify the emotion by finding the right language, we can more accurately identify the need affiliated with that emotion. When clients become familiar with these common needs it's like they find a missing puzzle piece. From there, relationships become easier and we find we have become more connected to ourselves and others.

Let's very much oversimplify emotions by categorizing them into two major groups. First, our "primary emotions" can be compared to roots of a tree, the underneath hidden part of ourselves. These emotions are deeper, more vulnerable, and can be difficult to express and be perceived by others. These emotions have the potential to draw others closer when we are able to share them. Common

47

primary emotions include feeling hopeless, loved, scared, inadequate, helpless, shame, guilt, lonely, out of control, neglected, abandoned, resentment, and remorse. The second category of emotions is like the branches and leaves of our tree, the most noticeable parts. Secondary emotions are reactive, often shown to others, and more readily expressed. These emotions tend not to draw others closer. Common secondary emotions are anger, disgust, jealousy, frustration, embarrassment, overwhelm, discouragement, irritation, and annoyance. The essential learning here is when we find ourselves engaged in reactive secondary emotions, it is an enormous benefit for us to slow down and explore the root of those reactive emotions. It is important to voice the primary root emotions inspiring the reactive secondary emotions. For example, Jack, who is working to be more authentic in sharing his internal emotional experience with Lisa, has shifted from his reactive irritability and annoyance to voicing a primary emotion; for example, he might say "I am feeling inadequate in my new role at work," and "I am feeling helpless as my parents age."

We are going to follow Jack as he uses the Emotion Word List and discovers his affiliated needs. So far what we know about Jack is that he is working to communicate more openly with his wife when she inquires, "How are you?" or "How do you feel about _____?" We also know he has shifted from a reactive emotional response of annoyance and irritability to sharing his primary emotions of inadequacy and helplessness. He reports an ease in his new relationship with himself, which contributes to what his wife reports as a "new chapter in getting to know Jack and understanding what he may need from me." Jack and his

YOUR RELATIONSHIP WITH **You**

wife have created new rules they live by in which "fine" and "ok" are no longer acceptable answers when someone who loves you is seeking to connect.

It may be helpful to download your own copy of the Emotion Word List and the Needs List (explained below) to have on hand for the next section of this chapter. If you are not able to do this, you can use the information provided within the chapter. For your downloadable copy, visit DeniseOnofrey.com/strategies-for-you

How the Emotion Word List works: we typically use go-to emotion words to describe our states. You'll find them in bold capital headers below. From there, I offer you a list of synonyms of varying degrees that will help you decipher a more accurate feeling than the go-to emotion word in bold. These aren't written in stone, and there isn't a right answer per se, but the tool will give you an opportunity to more accurately articulate how you feel. Remember, your go-to emotions, those secondary emotions, tend to be more overt and noticeable but not particularly connecting to others. On the other hand, primary emotions are more like underlying roots of secondary emotions which, when expressed, can connect us to others because we tend to be more vulnerable and authentic in expressing primary emotions. Ideally, by becoming familiar with our tendencies of emotional expressions, we will be more apt to express the primary, more connecting emotion.

Jack (husband, father, physician, triathlete), recently relocated to Boulder, Colorado from overseas. He is in a new management position at a preeminent hospital. Jack once reported that he was "happy" his sons are adjusting well to their new country, school and neighborhood. He was also "happy" to be among elite athletes in Colorado for upcoming competitions, which was a piece of his identity he could not fulfill while overseas.

Upon using the Emotion Word List, Jack now accurately reports he is <u>elated</u> his sons' adjustment is a positive one, as his first concern was the impact the move could have on the boys. In addition, Jack reports being <u>exhilarated</u> by the opportunities he has for his athletic pursuits.

Emotion Word List sample for HAPPY:

HAPPY—strong: thrilled, ecstatic, overjoyed, excited, <u>elated</u>, sensational, <u>exhilarated</u>, fantastic, terrific, turned on, euphoric, enthusiastic, delighted, marvelous, great.

HAPPY—moderate: cheerful, light, serene, wonderful, up, aglow, in high spirits, jovial, elevated.

HAPPY—mild: glad, connected, satisfied, gratified, pleased.

Jack was feeling <u>fearful</u>, a primary emotion, in relation to the move which was motivated by his parent's failing health. Jack did not feel he could express this fear because he felt responsible for uprooting his family and career to care for his parents. He did not think he had a right to be fearful. Among further exploration, he was able to tell his wife Lisa he was feeling a sense of <u>dread</u> and was <u>anxious</u>. Lisa was feeling the same way but wasn't sure she should share this with Jack because he was <u>apprehensive</u> about the move. The couple reported a deeper connection as they began to share emotions they had been suppressing.

The Emotion Word List sample for FEARFUL:

FEARFUL—strong: terrified, frightened, intimidated, horrified, desperate, panicky, dread, vulnerable, paralyzed.

FEARFUL—moderate: afraid, scared, apprehensive, jumpy, shaky, threatened, risky, alarmed, awkward, defensive.

FEARFUL—mild: nervous, anxious, unsure, hesitant, timid.

Jack's driving motivation to move was to ensure his parents received the medical attention they required. Lisa respects Jack's sacrifices for his parents. Until we explored this further, Jack assumed Lisa was being so amenable to the move because she had little choice given how dire her in-laws situation was. Once we opened up the conversation and I sought a more accurate description, Lisa was able to express that her affection toward Jack increased because of his admirable sacrifice for his parents. Jack was floored because what he thought was a bad thing for his family was actually an opportunity to bring he and Lisa closer. Jack reported this fortified his adoration and respect for Lisa. It is clear this exercise was far more connecting for Jack and Lisa then simply acknowledging "I care for him or her."

Emotion Word List sample for "CARE FOR":

CARE FOR—strong: tenderness, affection toward, captivated, attached to, devoted to, adoration for, loving, infatuation, enamored, idolize

CARE FOR—moderate: cherish, fond of, regard, respectful, concerned for, hold dear, prized, taken with, trust, close to, admirable

CARE FOR—mild: warm toward, friendly, positive toward

Lisa had complained to a friend about Jack being shut down because he was providing only one-word answers to her questions, especially when she asked how he felt about the move. Lisa jumped to the conclusion he must be depressed. It was the only thing that made sense to Lisa. Jack denied depression, but could not provide any insight into what he was displaying to Lisa. Given the work and exercises the couple was actively pursuing, I encouraged Jack to use the Emotion Word List. Jack reported feeling <u>down</u> about leaving his beloved staff in his previous position and <u>grim</u> about having to face his parent's mortality. In addition, Jack expressed feeling <u>alienated</u> as the new leader of his staff because he had replaced a highly-respected physician who led the team for decades. Once Jack was able to use the word list to "find" his experience, he and Lisa could easily connect. This new rule converted the question "How is work going, Jack?" and his answer, "It's fine," to a more connected and rich exchange.

The Emotion Word List sample for DEPRESSED:

DEPRESSED—strong: desolate, dejected, hopeless, <u>alienated</u>, gloomy, dismal, bleak, in despair, empty, barren, grieved, grief, despair, <u>grim</u>,

DEPRESSED—moderate: distressed, downcast, sorrowful, demoralized, discouraged, miserable, pessimistic, tearful, weepy, rotten, awful, horrible, terrible

DEPRESSED—mild: unhappy, <u>down</u>, low, bad, blah

Here are the additional sections of the Emotion Word List for your use.

INADEQUATE—strong: worthless, good for nothing, washed up, powerless, impotent, crippled, inferior, emasculated, useless, finished, like a failure

INADEQUATE—moderate: whipped, defeated, incompetent, inept, overwhelmed, ineffective, lacking, deficient, unable, incapable, small, insignificant, unfit, unimportant, incomplete

INADEQUATE—mild: lacking confidence, unsure, uncertain

CONFUSED—strong: puzzled, bewildered, baffled, perplexed, trapped, confounded, confused, full of questions, in a quandary, befuddled, in a dilemma

CONFUSED—moderate: mixed up, disorganized, foggy, troubled, adrift, lost, loose ends, disconcerted, frustrated, in a bind, ambivalent, disturbed

CONFUSED—mild: uncertain, unsure, bothered, uncomfortable, undecided

HURT—strong: crushed, destroyed, ruined, degraded, pained, wounded, devastated, tortured, disgraced, humiliated, anguished, cast off, forsaken rejected, discarded

HURT—moderate: belittled, shot down, overlooked,, criticized, defamed, censured, discredited, disparaged, laughed at, maligned, mocked, used, shamed

HURT—mild: put down, neglected, overlooked, minimized, let down

ANGER—strong: furious, enrage, seething, outrage, burned up, pissed off, violent, hatred, bitter, galled, vengeful, hateful, vicious

ANGER—moderate: resentful, irritated, hostile,

annoyed, upset, agitated, mad, offended, mean, upset, vindictive

ANGER—mild: disgusted, bugged, turned off, put off

GUILT—strong: degraded, mortified, exposed, sick at heart, horrible

GUILT—moderate: lost face, demeaned, wrong

GUILT—mild: regretful, embarrassed, at fault

Now let's consider what Jack's emotions may be telling him about his needs by using the Needs List. It's far more connecting to identify the emotion, acknowledge it, and assess our needs based on a clearly articulated emotion.

In the sample of the work Jack accomplished, he reported the following emotions:

Elated

Exhilarated

Fearful

Dread

Anxious

Apprehensive

Affection

Admiration

Adoration

Respect

Down

Grim

Alienated

We cannot assign somebody's needs to them. It is for each individual in the relationship to determine their own needs. The list below is a guide for you to explore, question,

YOUR RELATIONSHIP WITH *You*

and ponder once you have identified your emotions about an experience. Also, use Jack's work as a guide for how to relate emotions to needs. Jack learned to name the emotion, "elated," then ask himself: "When I feel 'elated,' what do I have the urge to do/have/experience/need?"

How to use the Needs List

The Needs List is a simple list of possible needs related to your emotions. Basic human needs can be found below in bold. Next you'll find synonyms for the needs to assist you in more accurately identifying your needs. I have found my clients benefit more from seeing their needs on a list than from relying on their own vocabulary to articulate their needs.

Jack decided that his elation about his sons' positive adjustment to the move was reason to celebrate with a special family outing. His need was to add <u>meaning</u>, mark the occasion, and celebrate the successful move with his family.

Needs related to **MEANING**: awareness, celebration, challenge, clarity, competence, contribution, creativity, discovery, growth, hope, mourning, purpose, participation, self-expression.

Jack asked himself, "When I feel 'dread,' what do I need?" He understood his "dread" came from a concern about <u>wellbeing</u>. By exploring the needs list, he now knows he likely needs safety, touch, and movement when he feels dread.

Needs related to **PHYSICAL WELLBEING:** air, food, movement, rest, sleep, sexual expression, safety, shelter, touch, water.

Jack asked himself, "When I feel 'anxious,' what do I need?" Jack now knows that when he feels anxious, he needs space and independence.

Needs related to **AUTONOMY:** choice, freedom, independence, space, spontaneity.

Jack asked himself, "When I feel 'anxious,' what else do I need?" He now knows he needs empathy, affection and consideration when he feels fearful.

Needs related to **CONNECTION:** acceptance, affection, appreciation, belonging, cooperation, communication, closeness, community, companionship, consideration, empathy, inclusion, intimacy, love.

Jack asked himself "When I feel 'admiration,' what do I need?" He now knows he needs Lisa's presence so that she is available to connect with his admiration for her.

Needs related to **HONESTY:** authenticity, integrity, presence.

Jack asked himself "When I feel 'grim,' what do I need?" He now knows he needs laughter and music when he feels grim.

Needs related to **PLAY:** music, dance, laughter, humor, joy, sports.

Jack and Lisa have achieved a renewed connection and speak excitedly about the ease in their relationship. Jack improved the relationship with himself by working hard to identify his internal emotional experience and share that information with Lisa. Jack is also far more skilled at deciphering and communicating needs based on his internal emotional experience. Lisa was an active and engaged partner in the process who also gained a new skill set that allowed her to improve her relationship with herself. This couple became much more able to turn toward each other and connect to get their needs met once they learned how to improve their relationship with themselves.

Now it is your turn to practice what Jack and Lisa have implemented and used to create their own rules for their family. Use the Emotion Word List to identify how you feel in this moment. If you'd like to use this exercise to work through a particular situation like Jack did, I encourage that. Try to come up with three to five emotions regarding how you feel in this moment or regarding a specific situation.

1.
2.
3.
4.
5.

Use the Needs List to ponder what the emotions you listed may be telling you about your needs.

Tips for using the Emotion Words List and the Needs List:

- Remember, this is not a hard science, so get comfortable with the grey areas of your emotions.
- What may be true for one person will not be true for everyone.
- It would be advantageous to use a calming strategy from Chapter Three to slow down, get quiet, and determine the best answer for you.

Jack lends his questions to guide you to your most authentic needs based on the five emotions you listed above.

1. "When I feel _____, what do I have the urge to do/have/experience/need?"
   Related need(s):
2. "When I feel _____, what do I have the urge to do/have/experience/need?"
   Related need(s):
3. "When I feel _____, what do I have the urge to do/have/experience/need?"
   Related need(s):
4. "When I feel _____, what do I have the urge to do/have/experience/need?"
   Related need(s):
5. "When I feel _____, what do I have the urge to do/have/experience/need?"
   Related need(s):

Investigating and articulating our internal emotional experience isn't easy. We tend to find all sorts of distractions from our emotions, or we oversimplify what we are feeling and rarely link specific needs to our emotions. This is due in large part because we are often limited in the words to accurately communicate our needs to ourselves and others. It is helpful to have a resource like the Emotions Word List and the Needs List at our fingertips. Be sure to download your own copies at: DeniseOnofrey.com/strategies-for-you

Key Learning:
- Emotions are the most reliable source of determining our needs.
- Working to identify emotions and learning what they are telling us will prevent us from getting

stuck in an unpleasant spot for too long.

◆ Each of us must be able to articulate our needs for more connection and ease.

◆ These lists help us "find" our experience on paper, which helps decipher our inner experience and needs.

5

THAT STUFF WE DO TO TUNE OUT

When we need to create calm and ease, we often use behaviors that aren't exactly ideal choices. I call these behaviors "ings," the behaviors we indulge in to calm and soothe ourselves when really, we are only tricking ourselves into fleeting moments of relief. When we "ing" we are distracted from what's going on inside of and around us. Why do I call them "ings"? To distract ourselves we often try working, drinking, Facebooking, exercising, eating, perfecting, primping, striving, planning, organizing, cleaning, shopping, or overdoing. Get the picture? Any behavior we're doing outside of healthy moderation is probably just distraction from what's going on inside and around us. "Ings" keep us from the best version of ourselves, and the best versions of our relationships. To take the bold step of living life by our rules, we must face the unconscious rules we follow by way of our "ings." Distraction is preventing us from dealing and healing from wounds; "ings" keep us in denial as we create noise and chaos between our daily lives and our truth. We "ing" to soothe, yet we actually create more noise and distraction from what is authentically happening in and around us. Listen, I get it. Relationships can be hard, being human can be hard, but I believe we are making it harder on ourselves at times (perhaps most of the time). I know I am guilty of it too. By staying distracted in all the noise of life and "ings," we are simply prolonging what we are avoiding. We must get real about our "ings" to live life by our rules. Somewhere along the way, we learned the rule to distract ourselves with "ings." It's time to buck the system and rewrite that rule.

A dear client of mine, "Celeste," a married mother of three, came to me in the early part of the year following a very chaotic holiday season. Celeste was clearly exhausted and reported that she was depressed, resentful, and "so over" all the demands of her life. Celeste's three school-aged children were involved in highly competitive gymnastics, requiring Celeste's involvement in chaperoning, carpooling, and meal planning for weekend-long trips to competitions. All of this kept her feeling, in her words, "on a constant high speed conveyor belt of doing s*** for other people." In addition, Celeste's husband traveled for work, and she felt burdened by the demands of keeping a household running, parenting, and some of the politics of her social groups.

Celeste is a classic "doer," an achiever, a "yes, yes, yes" person, all to ensure she is doing enough and is good enough. Celeste's *doing* gave her a false sense of safety and evidence that she was good enough. In addition, she was giving time and energy to organizations, her children's schools, her church, the gymnastic families, and being neighborly by providing childcare for the family next door whenever she was asked. Oh, and her parents recently moved to the neighborhood to "help with the children," but it wasn't working out as planned, and this became an additional stressor. So, at the end of the day, Celeste collapsed into bed with her head spinning, fearing she was forgetting things, and grappling with the urge to get out of bed and do more to make tomorrow "easier."

So, what's a woman like Celeste to do? She was exhausted, feeling resentful and overwhelmed by following rules in which she had to say "yes" in order to maintain her self-image and self-esteem. "Doing" and people-pleasing seemed to be a way Celeste ensured everything was ok and she was enough, she was "being good." Celeste was temporarily soothing a nagging thought that she was not good enough. She drowned out that thought with the chaos of doing. She proudly ran a constant list in her head of all she had accomplished in a day to (supposedly) feel calm and soothed—it was her drug of choice. From saying yes to neighbors and carpools that did not help her in return to providing meals for other families during her kid's competition weekends, Celeste was the kind of women we are impressed with and wonder, "How does she do it all and so well?" Did I mention that Celeste's appearance is nearly impeccable? As she sat across from me in my office, I even wondered how she does it all. This leads me to her other "ings."

Celeste indulged in private "ings" to deal with the draining impact of all her doing, striving and planning. Celeste's private getaway at the end of most nights of the week when her husband was away on business, was consuming alcohol, which, according to her, was "an amount I'm not OK with," coupled with excessive online shopping. When Celeste started working with me she knew this habit was part of the problem, but she kept the facts from me for quite some time. Despite the trust we built, Celeste later remarked she was embarrassed, ashamed, and guilty for the way she secretly behaved. Celeste reflected on her secret nightly habits with a dream-like glow, remarking how great it felt to "not give a care," "be rebellious" and "stick it to all the people I was perfect for every day." Celeste experienced a brief and temporary sense of calm and soothing that was not sustainable. Celeste was balancing her long days of exhausting "ings" with long nights of destructive "ings" to distract herself, creating more noise and chaos. The physical and emotional impact of drinking coupled with the stress of spending too much was incongruent with her values, her truest self, and the life she had planned. Also, because of all the purchase deliveries constantly arriving, yet another "ing" developed: hiding credit card statements and insisting on taking care of the family's finances. This not only added to her list of things to do, but was also deceptive toward her husband.

Celeste's nighttime "ings" created a cycle of shame, regret, and not feeling good enough, so by day she attempted to quiet that cycle by doing, striving and planning. She was left drained and wanting to throw reason out the window and break out of "being a perfect everything." Celeste compounded her exhaustion with little sleep, nighttime drinking, and shopping unnecessarily, only to wake up tomorrow and do it all over again.

In part, Celeste's truth—what she was avoiding—was disconnection from her husband; she suspected an affair but did not want address it "in case it is true." Celeste got honest about the impact of unresolved childhood trauma that was re-triggered when her parents moved to the neighborhood and had more access to her children. Lastly, when Celeste stopped distracting herself, she got very honest about what she valued, where she truly wanted to put her time and energy, and who she wanted to be giving it to. Celeste was beginning to rewrite her rules and concluded she only wanted to give to her immediate family in the foreseeable future. Once she recalibrated to the new rules, perhaps she would consider other areas to give, but with more discernment.

Ponder the "ings" you're indulging in to soothe and calm yourself, but instead only distract you. Getting clear on your "ings" may take some time while going about your everyday life in the habits that have previously gone unexamined. Use the list below and give some thought to your own "ing" habits. Remember, these are behaviors we engage in to calm and soothe, but are only distracting us from what is really going on in and around us. They may be behaviors you show others or keep private.

Shopping	Judging	Perfecting
Working	Eating	Emailing
Exercising	Drinking	Texting
Cleaning	Drugging	Go-go-going
Organizing	Gaming	Primping

Facebooking	Planning	Under-doing
Raging	Zoning out to TV	Overdoing
Complaining	Performing	Online Dating/
One-Upping	Proving	Searching

Are any of your "ings" not listed above? Add additional "ings" here:

_____

_____

_____

Let's dive a little deeper into your "ings" and why you "ing" the way you do. Listen, we are all doing it. Some of us are engaged in more or less extreme behaviors compared to Celeste. Either way, let's not consider "ings" as a weakness or a broken part of us. Let's consider our "ings" as an indication of where we can indulge in better care of ourselves and our relationships. "Ings" also indicate where we have an opportunity to take control over our time and energy and where we have an opportunity to write new rules to live by.

What behaviors do you engage in to create noise and distraction? Celeste engaged in doing and striving in many areas of her life, leaving others impressed and in awe at how she did it all. What parts of you do you hope no one sees or knows about? Celeste hid the drinking and shopping, which served as a rebellious relief and distracted her from disconnection, fear, and unresolved trauma. Use the prompts below to explore your "ings," their purposes, and to begin considering how you want to rewrite the rules you have been following. If you are going to take the bold step of living life by your rules, you must face the "rules" you unknowingly follow by way of your "ings." These prompts can help to get your thinking and discovery juices flowing.

"When I am honest with myself, I know my "ings" include the following…"

Celeste wore a mask throughout the day by way of her cheerful, overachieving helper role that was privately draining her and creating resentment she turned inward.

"I wear a mask by…"

Celeste wore her mask to appear like a good mother. Celeste had created a rule that if she was a doer, she was a good mother. Celeste's "ing" provided her a false sense of assurance.

"I wear this mask because there seems to be a rule that I…"

Celeste wore a mask by day with gymnastic families, her church community, social circle, and to her husband related to her drinking and their finances. "I wear a mask around this person or group of people…"

"I "ing" to avoid these emotions (use the Emotion Word List in Chapter Four)…"

Using the Needs List in Chapter Four, begin to write the new rules about your "ings." Until now, Celeste's covert rule had been that if she engaged in overdoing by day, she would have a sense of safety with evidence she was good enough. By night, Celeste's covert rule was she could be soothed and have ease, thanks to her well-deserved drinking and spending. We can see how Celeste's rules had resulted in the exhaustion, depressive symptoms and burnout. By addressing her needs, Celeste began to rewrite the rules she lived by.

Celeste had arrived at my office declaring her Plan A was not going as she had originally intended. Using the Needs List in Chapter Four, Celeste began to write the new rules. These rules fulfilled Celeste's needs for a purpose that she was falsely finding by overdoing for people who proved to be unhelpful to her in her times of need. Celeste began to add more movement in her day as well as a bedtime yoga practice to contribute to quality sleep. By creating a new rule around who she is willing to give her time to, Celeste began meeting her needs for autonomy, choice, and freedom, which she had been fulfilling by way of her rebellious drinking and shopping. Celeste created a new rule about discovery, growth and connection by creating goals in therapy to address her childhood trauma and disconnection from her husband.

Ponder the "ings" you're indulging in to soothe and calm yourself but that instead simply distract you. Use the "ings" list to examine your habits. Remember, these are behaviors we engage in to calm and soothe, but are only distracting us from what is really going on in and around us.

Key Learning:
- "Ings" are the behaviors we indulge in to calm and soothe ourselves.
- "Ings" are distracting and cause more noise.
- Becoming aware of our "ings" helps us write rules of connection and ease based on our needs.

6

PSST! YOUR GUT HAS
SOMETHING TO SAY

We have all experienced seasons in our life when we have a "yes, yes, yes" attitude: yes to life, energy, events, requests, love, and the people around us. For Celeste, in recent years, "yes" felt powerful and reinforced her "How does she do it all?" image. It wasn't until she stepped back and looked at the quality of her time, experiences, and relationships that she realized her life was not what she had planned it to be. She found herself at events, with others, or fulfilling tasks that left her wondering "How the heck did this happen?" Celeste unknowingly followed a covert rule "To say yes is to be a good wife, mother and neighbor." It left her drained, unenthused, and resentful. Celeste's rules had clearly failed to create the art of balanced living from all the "yes-ing" she had done. Celeste had to learn the art of saying "no" to ensure she could remain connected—first to herself, then to her children and husband. Celeste also had to become open to feedback from others, which can be vulnerable. If she said "no," she might lose her value in someone's eyes. She learned that if this was the case, she needed to say no to having that person in her life. This can be a painful and uncomfortable process, but it led Celeste to rules about who gets to be in her inner (and more meaningful and fulfilling) circle of community and friends.

After fumbling through a few seasons of "yes, yes, yes," Celeste was learning to trust her gut more. The boundary of knowing your truest "yes" and truest "no" will lead you to being more connected to yourself and others, as well as to the right people, places and things. Celeste reports that learning the art of saying "no," based on her gut reaction, is probably the best gift she has given herself. So, why is it so hard for us to say no sometimes? People-pleasing, perfectionism, and other pressures from our culture lead us to the answer. Without the skill of knowing when, where, and to whom we should say no, we can be stuck with resentments, drained and overwhelmed with demands that don't feed us. For Celeste, it led to a rebellious relief in drinking and shopping.

Recently a friend posted on Facebook, "How can I get to my own answer when I have so many other people's influence and opinions?" My advice to her was to ask her own gut. Her gut knows everything she needs to know. And so does *yours*! How relieving is that? Your "yes" and "no," your truest response, is already in you. Trust me. Trust your gut.

How does the strategy of saying "no" make relationships more connected and easier? Relationships get disconnected and hard for an array of reasons. One of the big ones is that when we are "yes (wo)men," we aren't living connected to ourselves. When we say yes in order to be accepted, to please others, or to avoid the discomfort and fear related to "no," we are stifling our gut's voice. We are ignoring our "knowing." There are fears we will miss out, be considered difficult, or appear selfish if we aren't pleasing others. The truth is, we must rein in, like Celeste did, and fine tune the art of when to say yes or no in order to be connected to ourselves first. Celeste found saying yes to herself resulted in physical movement, more time, healthy sleeping habits, and recovery from childhood trauma, all of which contributed to her resilience and capacity to address disconnection and dis-ease in her marriage.

At times, we have so much noise in our lives, environment, and in our own heads, we may not even be able to hear our gut, making our truest answer, our yes or no, so muffled that our gut's voice may seem silent. The truth is, we all have a gut reaction to guide us and help us get to our answers. Our gut reaction isn't particularly thoughtful; it does not calculate or weigh options, so there's less for us to do— glorious! Our gut reaction is simply what we know to be true. It is who we are at our foundation, our deep knowing that is not swayed by outside influences, noise, or pressure to please.

In my years of working with clients behind closed doors, I have created four essential strategies to practice quieting the noise and turn up the volume on our gut, which ushers us toward our truest selves. Beyond using these strategies for a "yes" or "no," you can use these strategies to write your new rules to live by based on what your gut says. Here are four strategies to practice hearing your gut and getting to your truest answers:

1. Get quiet: Hear your own thoughts, hear your own knowing, hear you. Celeste reports her head could be so loud and full, she dreamt of running away from the city and getting to nature. This fantasy is often just that, an escape fantasy in response to stress, overwhelm and noise. Depending on how loud the noise was in her head, the fantasy of running away from home was sometimes forever, a weekend, or at least for the day. What Celeste knew to be true: A) urges to run away, leaving her family, flaking on an obligation, or ignoring household tasks is a signal she needs to create her own quiet, and B) creating her own quiet is the antidote to the volume of noise in her head. Finding one minute a day for some form of quiet is essential for hearing yourself and living more connected and with more ease. There are a variety of ways to create quiet: find a favorite song, read a poem by a great like Maya Angelou, commit to sitting in the car for one minute prior to walking into work or the house, let your morning shower extend an extra minute and simply be quiet. Just a minute a day will do. Refer back to Chapter Three for more on this.

2. Discernment: Learning what is truly a problem to solve, versus what is simply your brain picking up a problem to chew on, is the second strategy I share with clients. Our brains are wired to seek solutions whether there is a problem or not. From a primitive perspective, our brains were developed to forage for food, stay safe, seek shelter, and reproduce. That's it! Fast forward to today; we no longer need to be in a constant loop of survival thinking to meet basic primitive needs. However, our brains don't completely understand that we can chill the heck out! For the most part our food, water and shelter is figured out and we don't need to constantly solve these problems. Our brains sort of pick up problems to soothe the urge to solve big issues and to put our gifts of survival to use. In today's times, we are constantly picking up problems to solve because it is our brain's tendency. However, this does not mean we must give in to this noise-producing tendency. Noise cancels out our gut's voice and we will be served by cancelling out the noise. It is our job to decide for ourselves: is this a noise-producing problem or a real problem to chew on?

3. *Talk, Write, Sleep:* Talk about what your gut is saying to you, or at least what you think it is saying. Hearing your own voice (your own wisdom) is powerful and informative. Even more powerful than talking with a trusted friend is talking aloud and listening to yourself. I encourage you to take the intimate step of being your own trusted confidante. Using a recording app on your phone to talk out your thoughts is a good way to hear what your gut is telling you. Listen immediately or take some space from the recording and return to it later. You will hear your own gut and your own answers. It works. You may notice yourself talking yourself out of what your gut is saying—this is your brain getting in the way. Too much brain and not enough heart, soul, and gut will tip the scales. You can *think* yourself right out of your wisdom and your gut's truest reaction. Are you interested in taking this strategy to the next level? While recording your voice on an app, use a mirror to look at yourself. Taking an intentional look at yourself in the mirror is a powerful gesture and creates connection to the self.

Another tool to hear your own gut is to write what it is telling you. Step away, and then go back to your written word. Not a pros and cons list (that's your brain using logic)—simply write out your thoughts and feelings so they are not spinning around in your head. Lastly, "sleep on it" is good old-fashioned advice that really works. Once you have heard or read what your gut is telling you, let your brain meld your inner wisdom to fortify the results. As mentioned earlier, our brains are wired to solve problems, but it is in our sleep that our brain can do its best work. While sleeping, our brain is without distraction from external forces, like your boss tapping your shoulder or a nagging to-do list. Talk, write, then sleep on your gut's thoughts and words. Your truest answers and truest self are in you 24/7. It is time to leverage *you* and reduce the noise.

4. Get clear and document your intention: Remember Celeste's escape fantasy of running away from the city and getting to nature? It was a positive reaction; it was her gut reaction to stress, overwhelm, and the noise in her head. It was a sign she needed to listen to herself. It is important that we take these messages seriously; it is critical that we be intentional and preventative about how we tend to ourselves and how we spend our time and energy. Preventative ways to tend to yourself include nature, walking around the neighborhood, listening to music, cooking a healthy meal, drinking more water, sipping on tea, or connecting with a friend. We must get clear, document our intentions, and use them as guideposts on how to tend to our truest selves. Celeste has a Post-It note on her bathroom mirror and in her car with the words, "Do you need nature?" This simple reminder helps her assess her stress and provides a solution if her stress is too high. Simply said, fantasy reactions to stress, overwhelm and noise are fantastic preventative medicine. What is your fantasy reaction to stress? Celeste once fantasized about drinking and online shopping. Now Celeste checks with her gut about what she needs. Celeste walks outside every day, does bedtime yoga, and has added more music to the home. I've asked my clients what their go-to escape fantasy reaction to stress is; here are some of their top desires:

- 10 minutes of music full blast, windows down, radio up!
- hot bath and candles
- going for a run
- hot meal prepared for me
- weekend with my sister
- perspective shift so I can feel how blessed I am
- quiet hug with a loved one
- someone telling me it will be ok

What is your go-to fantasy reaction to stress? What is your go-to when you are stressed, overwhelmed, and the noise in your head is maxed out? The answers to these questions are the first steps to hearing yourself. The next steps are working small doses of your fantasy into your daily life. Celeste can't run away from the city every day without detrimental impacts, but she can listen to sounds of nature during her bedtime routine or in the car between kid drop-offs. She can sit outside in the sun for 10 minutes and use her imagination to get away from it all.

What is your go-to fantasy when you are stressed, over-whelmed, and the noise in your head is maxed out?

What are smaller doses of this fantasy you can give yourself every day?

What will you do for yourself once a day to quiet the noise in your head?

What will you do for yourself every week to ensure you are indulging in a version of your fantasy?

I cannot express enough how essential it is to hear yourself by either recording your voice or reading your own responses, so I am adding some bonus material for you. There are 10 prompts below. That's 10 minutes of practicing what we just learned. Maybe set aside time now, or do a prompt a day for 10 days.

The more you turn toward yourself, listen to your gut, and honor what it is telling you, the more clarity you will have about you, your relationships, work, money, sex, needs, fun, dreams, and hopes. The more clarity you have, the more connected and easier both your relationships and your overall life will be.

Here are your 10 prompts. Write or record for a full minute, even if the initial answer only takes a few seconds.

1. What I know to be true (about me, you, relationships, sex, money, family, work, fun):
2. How I want to feel in my life (use the Emotion Word List in Chapter Four):
3. My time is best spent by:
4. The future excites me because: (or, my future would excite me more if _____ was in place/different)
5. What I love about me:
6. My proudest moment so far:
7. Today is a blessing because:
8. I am admired/loved/cared for because:
9. I am at my best when:
10. What I would never change about myself:

This chapter is jam-packed with why and how to get quiet and clear on what your gut has been pining for you to hear. What you learn from yourself about yourself will give you discernment, insight, and, of course, connection and ease.

Key Learning:

- Our gut reaction is our best answer to many questions.
- Our gut reaction helps us create balance, connection and ease.
- Noise and distraction muffle our gut's voice.
- Get quiet, discern which problems are worth your time and energy. Talk, write and sleep to hear your gut.
- Document and intentionally add doses of your go-to escape fantasy to daily living.

7

CHUCK IT IN THE F*&#-IT BUCKET

Introducing the "BUCKET!" This little gem is where you mentally put all the stuff that just doesn't really matter, yet drains you significantly, distracts you, and makes your life noisy, busy, and disconnected. It will help you take control, reduce demands, and conserve yourself for what really matters. This strategy will provide freedom, discernment, and empowerment. Once you get in the habit of using the Bucket, you will have more clarity, time, and energy. You write the rules, so you get to decide what to put in your Bucket.

"Bucket Items" are inconsequential nags and demands that seem to impact your mood, thinking and outlook. These important elements of our wellbeing can be improved by using this mental exercise. Bucket Items are not nearly as significant as their impact; they are self-imposed rules, expectations and standards. Bucket Items often feed your negative self-talk.

Here's one of my favorite examples of using the Bucket. My client "Rachel" is a good mom, wife, sister, and friend. She's just a ball of energy, she has the best laugh, and she is truly a gem of a person. Despite all her wonderful traits, she found a foolproof way to engage in negative thinking, thus altering her mood and outlook. Rachel calls it "The Room," and it represented her urge to deprive herself of fully being connected and at ease in the present moment. Rachel let this one room in her house—a large storage closet in the basement—nag her, drain her, and keep her from being fully at ease. This disorganized room took her mind, her focus, and her attention away from all of her wonderful attributes. Rachel had an endless supply of "shoulds" related to The Room: she should find time to organize it, should get rid of half the contents, should have never let it get so out of control. "Shoulds" are a signal you have a potential Bucket Item. Rachel described how she would have private thoughts of praise or satisfaction about herself and her accomplishments, but would quickly switch lanes to thinking about The Room, which made her feel badly about not being good enough. No matter where Rachel was, who she was with, no matter the degree of ease and connection she was feeling, she could automatically switch her thinking to The Room. This "evidence" that she was not good enough made her feel dread and instantly switched her outlook from positive to negative. For this super woman, The Room was kryptonite for connection and ease.

My heart broke for Rachel as she described her habit of using The Room to deprive herself of engaging in the present moment and experiencing connection and ease. We all do this in one way or another. We all deprive ourselves of feeling good about ourselves and allow something like a storage closet to put us in our place and drain us, reinforce our negative thoughts, and alter our mood and outlook.

Once Rachel identified The Room as an inconsequential nag that drained her, one that created noise and distraction, she was able to simply practice letting go of this thinking habit. (Chapter Eight is devoted to leveraging the brain's power.) Rachel simply noticed, "Oh, I am thinking of The Room," then reframed the thought of The Room to praise herself about something in the present moment. The present moment is where connection and ease reside. Having already taken the power from The Room by identifying it and acknowledging how her thoughts, mood, and outlook were altered, Rachel was already rewriting the rules she lived by. She no longer let an inconsequential nag like a room have power over her thoughts, mood and outlook. The Room went in the "F*&#-it" Bucket because it did not deserve any more power over Rachel. From there, Rachel found numerous self-imposed rules and standards that nagged and drained her. She uses the Bucket every day to stay the course and focus on things that truly matter. Rachel now has more power and control over her thinking, mood, and outlook. Other items Rachel chose to put in the Bucket:

- Battling kids to make their beds every day
- Balancing the checkbook
- Keeping her car spotless for carpool
- The guilt of saying "no"

Rachel decided each of these items were inconsequential and therefore robbing her of what matters most.

Let's figure out what you can put in the Bucket so you can have more power and control over your thinking, mood, and outlook. Remember, Bucket Items are self-imposed rules and standards that are inconsequential and unimportant in the big picture, but they impact our thinking, mood, and outlook. Hint: Bucket Items are often "should" statements. For example, Rachel "should" find time and energy to organize The Room.

Here are some areas where we may find Bucket Items. Review the list and notice what "should" thoughts come up for you. Take note of what emotions the "should" statements evoke in you. Notice how the "should" statements and accompanying emotions alter your outlook about the future.

Here's Rachel's example:

"Should" statement (thinking):

I should: **"Stop reading this novel and go clean The Room"**

Mood (what emotion does this "should" statement evoke?):

"Frustrated, defeated, grumpy, agitated"

How did the "should" statement alter your outlook about the future in this area? **"I will never get a handle on this house, it's too overwhelming."** Rachel is no longer enjoying her novel.

- Intimate relationships
  "Should" statement (thinking):
  I should_____

Mood: what emotion does this "should" statement evoke? It may help to use the Emotion Word List in Chapter Four

_____

How did the "should" statement alter your outlook about the future in this area?

_____

- Parenting, relationships with children
  "Should" statement (thinking):
  I should_____

  Mood: what emotion does this "should" statement evoke?

  _____

  How did the "should" statement alter your outlook about the future in this area?

  _____

- Body image
  Should statement (thinking):
  I should_____
  Mood: what emotion does this "should" statement evoke?

  _____

  How did the "should" statement alter your outlook about the future in this area?

  _____

Additional areas to explore include rules, expectations, and unhelpful drains and nags for the Bucket. Note your "shoulds," mood/emotions, and outlook related to:

- Relationship with parents
- Health
- Home, housekeeping, organization
- Work, success, relationships at work
- Community, volunteering, involvement, contribution
- Faith community
- Emotional, mental health, personal development

You may notice patterns in your Bucket Items as well as in the mood and outlook the items evoke. Consider what you learned in Chapter Two about overt and covert rules and expectations, namely how rules and expectations develop and how we unknowingly follow them. As you embark on writing your rules to live by, use The Bucket to edit out inconsequential nags and drains.

Be intentional. List three Bucket Items you are going to mentally practice putting in The Bucket as they arise in your daily life. Like Rachel, simply notice when you are engaging in an item that alters your thinking, mood, and outlook. Use the outcomes of the exercises above to raise your awareness about what items you are most likely to engage in. When you engage in a Bucket Item, reframe the engagement as an opportunity to praise yourself about something in the present moment.

Chuck these items in the F*&#-it Bucket:

1. _____
2. _____
3. _____

By intentionally putting your Bucket Items into your Bucket, you are declaring who is in charge of your wellbeing. The nags that drain you have had too much power over you and keep you from the present moment until now. Using The Bucket, you will have more freedom, discernment and empowerment. By using The Bucket, you will have more clarity, time and energy.

Key Learning:
- ◆ Bucket Items feed our negative self-talk.
- ◆ Bucket Items keep us from the present moment.
- ◆ Using The Bucket highlights what matters most.

8

GETTING YOUR BRAIN IN ON IT

We are far more important, powerful, and significant than we give ourselves credit for! The solution is in our thinking. We are going to write new rules to live by to challenge unhelpful thinking patterns, create new patterns, and reinforce what is already working. This three-step strategy will increase connection and you will have more ease with yourself and others.

Here's some bad news. Many of us are wired to think, and therefore feel, that we are inadequate and to believe we need improvement. Our wiring is reinforced by our culture, social media, and other factors such as overt and covert rules. The wiring process is complex and multi-layered; however, with simple strategies, we can harness our brainpower to rewire and leverage our new rules.

We live during a time of striving, doing, improving, and productivity. We seem obsessed with bettering everything as if this is the answer to connection and ease. For example, my client "Katherine" struggled to combat an ever-present thought that she should be better. Katherine laments that her job could have been more prestigious, her body could be in better shape, and her social circle was not what other people seemed to have. Katherine woke up every morning with dread, even though she reported she was grateful for her good and full life. Katherine was nagged by beliefs of not being good enough and by thoughts that she should be doing more to better herself. By challenging her automatic negative thinking and replacing it with positive thinking, Katherine was able to shed the emotional and mental weight of not following ingrained rules and expectations related to her career, body image, and social life, to name only a few. When I started working with Katherine, I asked her what I ask all my clients: "What will be different when we are finished working together?" She responded, "Honestly, everything. I need to change everything about myself and my life." (Keep Katherine's generalized thought in mind as we learn about the brain later in the chapter.) Katherine shared that she was not the lawyer she assumed she would be and had been groomed to be since high school and through college. Though she wisely and consciously decided instead to work in banking, Katherine had persistent automatic negative thoughts that she could always rely on to feed the anxiety that she wasn't good enough. Katherine's automatic negative thoughts about her career included, "I would not be as miserable if only I had become a lawyer," and "I should have just become a lawyer like I was supposed to, I bet I'd be happier." These thoughts easily generalized from her job to her body image and her small, though solid, group of friends. In fact, at one point Katherine shared, "I bet I would be in better shape if I was a lawyer... probably have more fun with friends, too." Katherine's voice trailed off as she was gaining insight into her automatic negative thinking. Katherine quickly added, "Wait! What am I saying? Being a lawyer, my body image, and my social scene aren't really related!" This is a great example of our brain's network of neurological pathways and the power of generalization. As soon as our brain "goes there" with a negative automatic thought, following the neurological pathways related to not being good enough, we can easily list off all the other ways we don't feel good enough. When we are operating from a neurological pathway of more *positive* thoughts, those positive-thought pathways generalize to other positive-thought neurological pathways. Simply put, we can engage in a web of neurological pathways to think negatively or positively. In addition, depending on which pathways we are operating from, we interpret other's actions, words and opinions via the same pathway. The implications on relationships are significant. This is key to understanding what we each bring to the Relationship Table: our own brain plays an essential role in how we interpret others.

Getting Your Brain to Do the Work

Hang in there with me as we learn a little bit about neuroscience and how it can help you let go of your automatic negative thinking. Neuroplasticity is our brain's ability to reorganize by forming new neurological pathways depending on which pathways are "exercised" with our thoughts. We truly can create change at the brain level to impact every facet of our lives. We now have promising science and methods allowing us not only to treat strokes, brain injuries, and dyslexia but also to improve the quality of relationships with self and others. Our thinking influences whether we intend to do something or not—our power lies in our intention. We have the power to put our brains to great use instead of passively falling prey to our negative thinking. Our brains are constantly renewing themselves; sometimes the brain is reinforcing positive thoughts and, too often, the brain is reinforcing negative thoughts. In fact, the brain has a natural tendency to hold on to negative experiences more often than positive ones. Attending to negative self-talk such as "I am not good enough," "I cannot get what I want," and that old nag, "Life did not turn out as planned," is up to you! Let's learn how to shift your brain to more positive thoughts, let go of others, and rewire what we once felt was stuck.

It's Like Brain Surgery But in Three Steps

Step One: Pause and notice

Notice and pause. Simply notice your self-talk habits—the first step to any change is awareness. By now this book has already stirred up some thoughts about how you talk to yourself about yourself, your relationships, and experiences in your life. Take a few moments to get quiet and honest about the negative self-talk you regularly indulge in.

If you aren't able to access your negative self-talk now, I want you to notice it in your daily life when something is frustrating, sad, "off," overwhelming, or fear-inducing. It is at these times that our automatic negative thoughts can become more obvious.

My personal example of awareness about my own automatic negative thoughts is when I dropped a smoothie on the floor. The glass shattered into a million little pieces and sticky green smoothie seemed to cover every inch of my floor and walls. My automatic thought was "Grrrr! You're so stupid!" It struck me how terribly I spoke to myself.

I wondered what I would say if a guest in my home had made the same mess. I would likely assure my guest it was no big deal, we would clean it up and move on. If I can easily let a guest in my home off the hook, how is it I can call myself stupid for the same mess? From that moment, I began to recognize how often and under what circumstances this automatic negative thought arose.

Here are common automatic negative thoughts. You may hear your own voice in some of these statements. Make note of any that resonate with you, and begin to notice when and where you say these statements to yourself:

- I am not worth it
- I cannot speak up for myself
- I do not like myself
- I cannot trust myself
- I cannot share my feelings
- I am not wanted
- I cannot get what I want
- I will not succeed
- I cannot do it
- I am not good enough

This first step is all about awareness. Notice when and under what circumstances your brain automatically responds with a statement similar to the ones above.

Step Two: Standing up to yourself for yourself

You improve the relationship you have with yourself by challenging your automatic negative thoughts. Whether you believe it in the moment or not, I encourage you to practice attaching the opposite statement to your automatic negative thoughts. This practice will actually change your brain's neurological pathways.

Going back to my example of dropping a sticky green smoothie, my automatic negative thought popped up: "You are so stupid!" I began to speak to myself as I would to a guest in my home who made the same mistake: "You are so stupid! No, you're not, it was an accident. It can be cleaned up. No biggie. You are far from stupid, sister." This step works with your brain's natural and powerful tendency to reorganize itself with new neurological connections that will support a more connected and easier relationship with yourself. In addition, you will begin to interpret other's actions, words, and opinions through a lens to support a more connected and easier relationship. This is key: talk back to the automatic negative thoughts with opposite and kinder statements as if you are a guest in your home.

Step Three: Practice what is working

Ok, so I am shedding more light onto the inner workings of my own relationship with myself which feels vulnerable, but I am willing. Take my former automatic negative thought of "You are so stupid." One of the keys to my success in combating it is practicing praise when I feel opposite of "stupid." When I feel confident, wise, and grounded in what I know to be true, I privately practice encouraging myself to reinforce my positive thought's neurological pathways. Remember, with the gift of neuroplasticity, we have the power to change our brain's natural tendencies. By highlighting when I feel the opposite of "You're so stupid," I am literally fortifying these positive neurological pathways, thus influencing my relationship with myself and the lens through which I view and interpret others.

What automatic thoughts do you engage in?
1.
2.
3.

Under what circumstances do these automatic thoughts tend to pop up?
1.
2.
3.

What positive, self-encouraging, and sometimes opposite statement will you use to combat your automatic negative thoughts (as if you were a guest in your home)?
1.
2.
3.

Going forward, maintain awareness about when and where your negative automatic thoughts pop up. Combat your negative automatic thought by pairing it with a positive and sometimes opposite thought. Be sure to reinforce when you feel good, strong, and confident with encouragement so your brain's neurological pathways become strengthened. When we begin to free ourselves from repeating automatic negative thoughts, we enrich the relationship we have with ourselves and others. This chapter gave you three steps to challenge old patterns, create new patterns, and reinforce what is already working. You now have a new rule to live by: I combat my automatic negative thoughts with the kindness I offer guests in my home.

Key Learning:
- Actively combat negative automatic thoughts to diminish their power.
- Pair negative automatic thoughts with positive, kinder thoughts.
- Talk to yourself as if you were a guest in your home.
- Your brain's tendencies can be influenced by how you think and talk to yourself.

9

YOU'RE JUST A TALL BABY!

Don't be shocked, don't be insulted. I am just a tall baby, too. I say this to all my clients to help them make sense of what most of us are seeking in relationships. This applies to all relationships, from intimate to parenting to community.

Picture it: we were all born from a woman's body. We came into this world and it was bright, cold and overwhelming. Our senses were in overdrive; maybe we felt anxious, scared, bewildered, curious, and stressed. What an introduction to the world! Immediately, someone started to soothe us and make us feel better by talking to us and holding us. Chances are we were cleaned, poked, prodded, and swaddled. For many of us, we were laid on our birth mother's chest and we began to build relationships with those around us. We had needs, and those needs got met to varying degrees.

From that big day, someone took us home and continued to meet our needs to varying degrees. We started to formulate who our primary caregivers were. We started building T.A.B.S. (Trust, Assurance, Boundaries, and Safety) with others and the world around us. Our caregiver(s) reinforced our T.A.B.S. based on their varying degrees of accessibility, reliability, responsiveness, and engagement, answering the most basic of human needs and questions: "A.R.R.E (Accessibility, Reliability, Responsiveness, Engagement) you there for me?"

Here's a quick look at what each of the A.R.R.E. elements encompass when considering our relationship with ourself, adapted from the work of Dr. Sue Johnson:

Accessible: Are you open, willing, welcoming to yourself? Are you available to hear your gut reaction's voice?

Reliable: Follow-through, consistent, dependable, do what you say, a person of your word for you. Do you consistently provide your gut reaction an opportunity to be heard?

Responsive: Receptive, understanding, sympathetic, providing yourself grace, heeding the call for you. Do you adhere to your gut reaction's guidance?

Engaged: Involved, secured, actively pursue what feeds you, interested in you. Do you participate in calming and quieting practices to give your gut reaction a chance to be heard?

Fast forward: in adulthood, we move away from the caregivers we were born to and toward the big task of choosing our own caregiver (spouse, partner, husband, wife, etc.). Within our adult relationships, we are still those Tall Babies needing the same T.A.B.S. via A.R.R.E. We just happen to be taller and have more responsibilities, but our needs remain the same no matter our age. The needs in our adult relationships are as imperative and essential as the day we were born.

There is science to prove we are all just Tall Babies. Research tells us babies cannot thrive with only food, water, and shelter. Babies require a relationship with a caregiver in which s/he can feel T.A.B.S by way of a caregiver's A.R.R.E. And, you guessed it, you do too. No matter your age, level of responsibility, or whether you are a caregiver to children, you need T.A.B.S. through A.R.R.E. It is when we receive and provide T.A.B.S through A.R.R.E. that we are connected to others with greater ease.

Who in your life is accessible, reliable, responsive and engaged with you? Maybe it's one person, a group of people, a family member, a partner, a neighbor, a mentor, a congregation, or a coworker. More importantly, A.R.R.E. you there for yourself? When we tend to ourselves by being accessible, reliable, responsive, and engaged, we can more readily receive our needs and provide for others. In addition, we are building Trust, Assurance, Boundaries, and Safety with ourselves and the world around us.

Within every facet of your life, it is important to maintain your relationship with yourself by being accessible, reliable, responsive and engaged with yourself. Using the elements of A.R.R.E., consider the key areas of your life and the quality of your relationship with yourself.

Intimate relationships: How do you maintain access-ibility, reliability, responsiveness, and engagement with YOURSELF within intimate relationships? In other words, how healthy and strong is your relationship with yourself when you focus on maintaining or building a relationship with another? Mark items you are unsure of or leave unanswered as "Future Intentions." Future Intentions indicate areas where you may need to write new rules for yourself. Find examples of each element in parenthesis based on the work of my clients.

Accessible: *(e.g., I access my own gut reaction about relationship decisions)*

Reliable: *(e.g., I maintain my workout schedule even when my husband is on the road and I feel too busy)*

Responsive: *(e.g., When I want touch, I reach for my partner)*

Engaged: *(e.g., I keep track of goals for being a better me in my relationships)*

Parenting and Relationships with Children

How do you maintain accessibility, reliability, responsiveness, and engagement with YOURSELF within your parenting relationships? In other words, how healthy and strong is your relationship with yourself when you focus on your parenting role? Once again, mark items you are unsure of or leave unanswered as "Future Intentions." Future Intentions indicate areas where you may need to write new rules for yourself.

Accessible: *(e.g., I remain open and willing to see how I can parent more effectively)*

Reliable: *(e.g., I maintain the boundaries I set with my children)*

Responsive: *(e.g., I am most kind to myself on days parenting isn't going so well)*

Engaged: *(e.g., I actively journal no matter how tired I am at the end of the day)*

Health, Self-Care, Body Respect

How do you maintain accessibility, reliability, responsiveness, and engagement with YOURSELF within your health, self-care, and respecting your body? In other words, how healthy and strong is your relationship with yourself when you focus on a relationship with yourself in caring for your body? Mark items you are unsure of or leave unanswered as "Future Intentions." Future Intentions indicate areas where you may need to write new rules for yourself.

Accessible: *(e.g., I welcome opportunities to walk with my friends so I have a few different walking buddies in my neighborhood)*

Reliable: *(e.g., I consistently drink water throughout the day)*

Responsive: *(e.g., My doctor said no more coffee or colas, so I quit)*

Engaged: *(e.g., I ski every other Sunday with my family no matter the weather because it feeds me)*

Additional areas to consider elements of A.R.R.E. in your relationship with yourself:

- Relationship with parents
- Work, success, relationships at work
- Community, volunteering, involvement, contribution

- Faith community
- Emotional, mental health, personal development
- Social circles, gathering and social obligations

Use the insights gleaned from assessing your A.R.R.E. elements as a guide for where you are treating yourself well and where your Tall Baby may be feeling deprived. Just like there are no perfect parents, we can't be in perfect relationships with ourselves. However, we can make an honest assessment, consider new rules for ourselves, and bring forth a relationship of connection and ease. By treating ourselves with A.R.R.E. elements, we are building trust, assurance, boundaries, and safety with self, providing a litmus test for how other relationships should be.

In this chapter, you began to explore yourself as a Tall Baby. In Book Two of The Connection Strategy Book Series, we will delve deeper into how to apply what you learned here to your most important relationships. You will also learn how to apply your strengths in being accessible, reliable, responsive, and engaged with yourself toward creating more connected and easier relationships with others based on trust, assurance, boundaries and safety.

In the next chapter, we will re-examine key strategies to challenge the status quo, examine the rules we have been unknowingly following, and eliminate the noise and the distractions keeping us from connection and ease with ourselves. Finally, we will give our strategies some legs, fuel, and zest by writing our own rules to live by in our relationship with ourselves.

Key Learning:

- ◆ We have the same basic needs today as we did the day we were born.
- ◆ Trust, assurance, boundaries and safety are built into relationships with accessibility, reliability, responsiveness and engagement.
- ◆ We must connect and have ease with ourselves before we can turn towards others and expect the same.

10

INTENTIONALLY YOU BY <u>YOUR</u> RULES

So far, we have acknowledged the truth about some things in our lives not turning out as planned and the disconnection and lack of ease we may feel as a result. We learned how to begin shifting out of disconnection by slowing down, calming ourselves, and getting real about our emotions and affiliated needs. From there, we learned about some of the ways we cope with disconnection and being ill at ease that aren't working out for us in the long run. Next, we learned key strategies to reduce the noise and distraction keeping us from a connection and ease with ourselves, including listening to our gut, reducing inconsequential nags that drain us, and using our brain's natural power to reduce negative self-talk and fortify positive self-talk. Lastly, we were introduced to a way to look at our most basic needs; the food, water, shelter of our emotional selves: T.A.B.S. (Trust, Assurance, Boundaries and Safety) by way of A.R.R.E (Accessibility, Reliability, Responsiveness, and Engagement). We learned how to actively meet the needs for ourselves and others.

Maybe you will take away a few gems from *Your Relationship with You: How to Live Life by Your Rules* and hope the impact will work its way into your relationships with yourself and others. Perhaps you will make grand changes and put impressive effort into drastically revamping your relationship with yourself. Maybe you'll give yourself permission to do nothing for now. How about we meet somewhere in the middle by writing a few rules without tremendous overwhelm and noise? Let's create change by being A.R.R.E. with ourselves. Before we say goodbye and until we meet again in Book Two of The Connection Strategy Book Series, write your rules to live by for each of the areas we explored in Book One. Remember?

- Calming and slowing down
- Identifying emotions and affiliated needs
- Confronting "ings"
- Hearing your gut reaction
- Chuck It In the F*&#-it Bucket
- Leveraging your brain's neuroplasticity

It is important to not only strike while the iron is hot, it is also important to keep the momentum of new rules *at a pace that will ultimately serve you*. Taking on too much will eventually just create noise and distraction, leading you back to disconnection and lack of ease. Not taking on the challenge of writing new rules to live by will leave you in the status quo of noise and distraction, in disconnection and lack of ease. As you think back to Chapters Three through Eight where you learned key insights and strategies to write *your rules*, I want you to listen to your gut and decide which areas need the most attention. You may not need every strategy in this chapter at this point. You can return to this book at another time and find different, more suitable strategies.

Writing Your Rules to Live By

Here are essential steps to leveraging what we have learned in *Your Relationship with You: How to Live Life by Your Rules*:

1. Define your "why" for the new rule and what value the new rules will bring you.
2. Get clear about what you want. It is important we get calm in order to get clear so practice the strategies in Chapter Three "Slow and Calm Wins the Race."
3. Be specific about what you want, how you want to feel, and the impact you desire —this will help you craft rules worth your time and energy without creating noise and distraction.
4. Share your intention with someone you have T.A.B.S. with and who meets the "A.R.R.E. you there for me?" criteria. If you aren't sure who this is quite yet, simply continue being that person for YOU. That's the whole point here anyway!
5. Do something every day to demonstrate your commitment to your new rules.
6. Keep track and celebrate how well you are doing in your relationship with YOU.

7. Remember, this is about writing your rules and fine-tuning your relationship with you. This is about being accessible, responsive, reliable, and engaged with you. May your rules reflect the quality of relationship you will soon have.

Let's get some rules on paper.

My Rules to Calm and Slow Down

Calm is the foundation to connecting with ourselves and therefore helping us connect with others. Our state of mind is the foundation of our interactions, relationships, and experiences. We must learn to tap into calm for optimal outcomes. It is nobody else's job to calm you. Under most circumstances, it is our responsibility to calm ourselves. We are responsible for the degree and quality of connection in our lives.

1. My new rule about adding calm and slowing down:

2. I expect the rule of adding calm and slowing down to add value because I:

3. My commitment to calm and slowing down is to:

4. I will practice implementing this new rule everyday by:

5. I will keep track of my daily habit by:

6. I will share my intention for change with:

My Rules to Get Off the Emotional Merry-Go-Round

Emotions are the most reliable source of determining our needs and each of us must be able to articulate our needs for more connection and ease. Big emotional events happen along with the constant thread of emotions running throughout our days. We can get stuck in those emotions, especially when our needs go unmet. Working to identify emotions and learning what they are telling us will prevent us from getting stuck in that same spot for too long.

When we have an emotional experience, logic can just fly out the window. We lose ground, lose perspective, and just can't seem to get past the emotions. When we are not articulating our truest selves and our truest experiences, we are missing an opportunity to connect to ourselves and others.

1. My new rule to identify my emotions and their implied needs in my relationship with myself is:

2. I expect the impact of identifying my emotions and needs will be:

3. My commitment to emotional identification is:

4. Every day, I will practice implementing new rules by:

5. I will keep track of my daily rules by:

6. I will share my intention for change with:

My Rules About My "Ings"

To distract ourselves, we often indulge in working, drinking, Facebooking, exercising, eating, perfecting, primping, striving, planning, organizing, cleaning, shopping, and overdoing it. Any behavior we're doing outside of healthy moderation is in place because it's distracting us from what's going on inside and around us. When we are distracted from what is going on inside us and around us, we are keeping ourselves from the best version of ourselves and the best version of our relationships. Let's get real and commit to getting our "ings" within healthy moderation and look at what we have been avoiding.

1. Why I intend to create new rules and change regarding my "ings:"

2. I expect the impact of creating new rules and change regarding my "ings" to be:

3. My commitment to my new rule and change related to my "ings" is:

4. I will practice implementing new rules daily by:

5. I will keep track of my daily rule by:

6. I will share my intention for change with:

My Rules for Hearing My Gut Reaction

At times, we have so much noise in our lives, environment, and heads that we may not even be able to hear our gut, making our truest answer, our yes or no, so muffled it may even seem silent or non-existent. The truth is, we all have a gut reaction that can guide us and help us get to our answers. Our gut reaction isn't particularly thoughtful; it does not calculate or weigh options. Our gut reaction is simply what we know to be true. It is who we are at our foundation, free from outside influences, noise, or pressure to please. Let's create some rules and change that noise!

1. Why I intend to turn down the noise so I can access what my gut instincts are:

2. I expect the impact of having access to my gut instincts will be:

3. My commitment to myself is:

4. I will practice implementing new rules daily by:

5. I will keep track of my daily rules by:

6. I will share my intention for change with:

My Rules, My Bucket

Yes, THE BUCKET: where you mentally put all the stuff that just doesn't really matter, yet drains you significantly, distracts you, and keeps your life noisy, busy and disconnected. It's up to you to take control of what you can, reduce demands, and conserve YOU for you and for what really matters. How will you give yourself freedom, discernment, and empowerment with your Bucket? Once you get in the habit of using the Bucket, you will have more clarity, time, and energy.

1. Why I intend to use the Bucket to reduce drains, noise and distractions:

2. I intend to use the Bucket in the following areas of my life (work, parenting, household, morning, evening, dinner time, interactions, daily habits, sleep routine, health, body, friendships):

3. I know what should go in the Bucket immediately:

4. I expect the impact of the Bucket to be:

5. My commitment to using the Bucket is:

6. I will practice implementing new rules daily by:

7. I will keep track of my daily rule by:

8. I will share my intention for change with:

My Rules and My Brain

We must free ourselves from thoughts that do not serve us and fortify the positive thoughts that will give each of us TLC, empowerment, and clarity. This book was designed for you to explore and discover more about YOU, to connect and have more ease with yourself in order to turn toward others.

Chapter Eight taught you how to get your brain to let go of the thinking that hinders you and thereby increase the power of your best self. You were given three steps to challenge old patterns, create new patterns, and reinforce what is already working. This three-step strategy will increase connection and you will have more ease with yourself and others. Let's set some rules to get your brain in on your new rules.

1. Why I intend to use the three steps found in Chapter Eight, "Getting Your Brain in on It:"

2. I expect the impact of this strategy will be:

3. My commitment to using this strategy is:

4. I will practice implementing new rules daily by:

5. I will keep track of my daily rules by:

6. I will share my intention for change with:

Until We Meet Again

We are all shaped by our surroundings, by spoken and unspoken rules, our culture, and our perceptions of what we are supposed to be, do, say, feel, and pursue. I was inspired to write this book by the clients I work with every day. My clients have the opportunity to step back, explore, and discover the rules they have been following but that no longer fit.

The clients I work with design their own ways to show up to their lives. Most importantly, they add and eliminate factors keeping them from living the life they intended to live. I want us all to be more empowered to buck the system—the rut and the daily grind we all fall into simply due to the nature of life, demands, family, career, and so on. My mission has long been to help each of us to better indulge in the finer things in life: relationships, connection and ease. It is my belief that when we eliminate factors that create noise and distraction from what is going on in and around us, as well as add key strategies to live with more connection and ease, our relationship with ourselves will truly be our greatest asset.

Remember, we are all more important, powerful, and significant than we give ourselves credit for. We have been influenced by overt and covert rules and expectations that can leave us in a life we did not plan for. The key is knowing YOU have the power to rewrite the rules that no longer serve you. Once you rewrite the rules, you will gain more connection and ease, I promise you.

I trust that if you got this far in the book, you are already living differently and beginning to live by new rules. I believe in you. I believe you can live life by *your* rules with greater connection and well-deserved ease.

WHAT TO EXPECT NEXT

BOOK TWO
WE: RELATIONSHIP STRATEGIES
FOR CONNECTION

Now that you've finished *Your Relationship with You: How to Live Life by Your Rules*, you have a solid understanding of you and what you bring to any Relationship Table. Though what you bring is fluid over time and may change with different relationships, it is imperative to understand your "stuff" in order to turn toward others for more connected and easier relationships.

"We: Relationship Strategies for Connection" is Book Two of The Connection Strategy Book Series. It provides an in-depth understanding of your hard-wired needs, the impact on your life when your needs are not met, and it offers methods and exercises for getting your needs met. Book Two explains how to approach the Relationship Table and best navigate the relationship with our partners based on our own unique contributions. Next, Book Two empowers you and your partner to take the facts and nuances of your relationship and create your own relationship rules and rituals. Often, cultural pressures and expectations make our relationships difficult. So ask yourself, "What would it be like to buck the system and create your own relationship rules to live by?" Trust me, your own rules are much easier to follow. With this ease, you will have more connection.

Some clients have remarked they wish they had this know-how and these strategies from the start of their relationship, while others acknowledge the beauty of unfolding more intimate parts of themselves over time in the security of a long-term relationship. No matter the stage or age of your relationship, Book Two provides you and your partner with a common language and offers powerful tools essential for all relationships.

It is important to continue the quest to create your own rules to live by within your most important relationships. Once we have developed more connection and ease within ourselves, we are then more primed to enrich the relationships around us. Though at first glance Book Two may appear to be a couples' book aimed specifically at relationships of a romantic and intimate sort, you will be able to use Book Two for all kinds of relationships. The insights and information in both Book One and Book Two remain true for all relationships: the concepts, struggles and demands of all human interaction are consistent. Nearly every one of us is seeking ease and connection in all of our important relationships.

Book Two can be applied to home, work, extended family, and community relationships. For example, "Chloe" and "Rose" are middle-aged sisters. As adults, this sibling pair sought ways to create connection and ease in their

YOUR RELATIONSHIP WITH *You*

relationship and used the concepts in Book One, then followed up with the concepts in Book Two, to write new rules for their once-conflicted relationship.

A sample of what you will learn in Book Two includes how to:
- Dissect interactional patterns ("We are in a rut!") and learn ways to stop those patterns.
- Develop a "Relationship Playbook" for each member of the relationship.
- Understand the *real* inner workings of your relationship by examining, building, and leveraging Trust, Assurance, Boundaries and Safety.
- Move beyond "being there" for each other. Relationships with ease and connection have a deeper appreciation and mastery of Accessibility, Responsiveness, Reliability and Engagement.

121

ACKNOWLEDGMENTS

My editor Bobby Haas, who is as talented as he is patient, thank you for teaching me more about myself, the process and trust. My business strategist, friend and second brain Kimberly Alexander. My project manager Susie Schaefer for your loving kindness, input and for keeping me on track. Kurt for providing time, feedback and all that good stuff when I needed it most. My educators, supervisors and mentors of all types for making me into the professional I am today. My parents and grandparents for ensuring I know the value of education, loyalty and hard work. My sisters, extended family and all my sisters from another mister for being the best tribe a girl could ask for.